Lovesongs & Reproaches

PASSIONATE CONVERSATIONS WITH GOD

L. William Countryman

Morehouse Publishing
NEW YORK · HARRISBURG · DENVER

Copyright © 2010 by L. William Countryman

Morehouse Publishing, 4775 Linglestown Road,
Harrisburg, PA 17112
Morehouse Publishing, 445 Fifth Avenue,
New York, NY 10016

Morehouse Publishing is an imprint of
Church Publishing Incorporated

Cover design by Laurie Klein Westhafer
Cover art by Pene Brook
Interior design by Vicki K. Black

Library of Congress Cataloging-in-Publication Data
Countryman, Louis William, 1941-
Lovesongs and reproaches : passionate conversations with God / Bill Countryman.
        p.   cm.
ISBN 978-0-8192-2394-4 (pbk.)
1. Spirituality. I. Title.
BV4501.3.C68945 2009
242—dc22

                                    2009036055

Printed in the United States of America

11 12 13 14 15 16   10 9 8 7 6 5 4 3 2 1

For Jon, my spouse,
with whom I have learned much about love

Contents

And there was light

You there! Maker of all!
Why did you not do better?
Let there be light! Ah, yes,
the fireworks at the beginning were a good touch,
appealing to the ten-year-old in everyone.
But the working out of the details
has proved as much failure as creation.
Your resources are infinite,
but you cast half-finished works
aside as if you had no time
to bring them to perfection. Mars
circles the Sun, frozen
and dry. The mammoths are gone.
And just look at us!
We used to say we were the crown
of your work—much honor it did you!
Yes, we, ignorant, stupid,
petty, arrogant, cooperating
with evil when not inventing it
ourselves. Why did you not
do better? Do we ask so much?
To be safe from pain and disaster

and from one another, to have
what we need when we need it.
Call us self-centered, but do we
have a choice? We know
our limits—one life here
and then whatever's hidden
in your hand. Don't try
to buy us off with flashes
of beauty. The perfect sunrise
today only means
the drought continues and deepens,
not that the weeds in my garden
notice.

        Your choice of canvas—
that's the problem. Your canvas
was too small. This vast
universe is still too limited.
Every yes entails a no
somewhere. The clash, the conflict,
the competition shapes us who we are.
Evolution was a sloppy choice,
a clumsy tool. What could it do
but cobble monsters together,
leaving inside us scraps
of the past, fish-parts that fail
the demands of life in air?
Perhaps you thought it generous
painting your infinite vision
across this poor world, this patch

of clay. We live in the gulf
between the vision and your choice of medium.

Still, there *is* sunrise
in tones of gold and rose
with birdsong to welcome it.
Who can turn his back on it?
Who refuse the renewal of the day?

||

Outsized
Supernatural Bodies

In the old time, I think it was easier.
There was a god for everything,
small gods with one thing to do
and doing it well. Grant me
a holiday with Horace at the spring
of Bandusia, the sacrifice, the feast
to follow, the assurance of water,
clear and cold, whatever
the season. One thing to hold onto
for certain. *O fons Bandusiae,*
splendidior vitro! There was the war,
of course—and Horace on the wrong side.
But he came through all right.
Mars must have liked him—
and Augustus, himself a god-to-be.
    All right, I've fallen into the pit
of travel-writing: the romance
of being pampered for a week in foreign
places, other times.

No one dreams of being
a field slave on Horace's farm.
What god cared about them?
Better yet, we want to visit
Phoebus—his palace "lifted up
on towering columns...brilliant
with flashing gold, sleek
ivory covered the roofs,
wide doors gleamed with silver,
the artistry outdoing even
the materials." Yes, we
do remember that Phaethon came
to no good there. But we
will moderate our desires, stay out
of the solar stables, just
enjoy the view—and hope
no rival, jealous deity
has noticed us peering over
the balustrades at the world below.
        Oh yes! I know the danger.
Euripides taught me: a devotion
too single-minded, court
paid too exclusively
to one god among the many—
this endangers a mortal.
Artemis for the hunt, but
don't forget to honor
Aphrodite for her gifts
or you'll wind up like Hippolytus,

a torn mess of blood and bones,
lying in your chariot's wreckage.
     But superstitious folk never
lack for worries anyway.
How much is that "too much"
that transgresses a god's prerogatives?
Where to draw the line?
When to supplement the humble
service of Pomona on your farm
with offerings to the gods of state,
averting war and the tax collector?
And, for those of us kept safe
by some kind deity
(is it Hygieia?) from the curse
of paranoia, we know that, good
or ill, all comes from the will
of the gods, each governing
a separate sphere, sometimes
quarreling with each other,
sometimes taking revenge,
sometimes smiling, sometimes
colliding, with never a thought of whom
they've smashed between their outsized,
supernatural bodies.

III

Or Luck

Still, it was easier then.
At least, the intellectual labor
was less burdensome. We
were content with small gods, small
explanations, enough to know
that this weal, this woe came
from her, from him—and nothing
to be done. And the old gods
were little freer than we.
Constrained by fate and one another,
they must have learned detachment
of some sort. Artemis, in her last scene,
admits she cannot interfere
with Aphrodite's revenge,
bids her Hippolytus farewell
and leaves him alone to die,
a god's eyes being too pure to watch
the climax of mortality.

Who taught us to ask for more?
to seek a larger whole?
Plato, who made a system
of ideas? Or Alexander,

who made the whole world dream
of mimicking it in empire
and in stone, the stone of cities
and forts and palaces? Neither,
I think. I think it was you—
and the ceaseless, busy interaction
of all that you have made.

    We were unsure, of course,
who you might be. Were you
Fortuna, long rumored to control
the destinies of gods and mortals
alike? And was it true, then,
that you were beyond all worship,
immune to blandishment? No gambler
would ever think so. We chose
to take precautions. Why *not*
worship the Luck of Antioch
with temple, with rites, her image
on our coins? It can't hurt.
Hey! for centuries it seemed
to work. And then not.

    Too bad, but we couldn't just
go back to the old stories.
So Zeus was king of the gods?
Yes, but only king.
He never could get round
his wife in that business of Io.
You drove us to think bigger.

If Fate, Luck, Fortune
is what there is, so what?
An explanation that explains nothing.
There is no story there,
no Why. Only Democritus'
rain of atoms endlessly
catching on one another,
turning, wheeling, snagging,
producing meaningless clumps
only to part again.
Ah! the atom! yes!
Luck with a longer name.

IV

Who maketh the clouds his chariot

Who, then? We couldn't
start at the One and work
our way down the chain. The One,
the Monad, resists division
even in the mind.
How to connect the ideal, the imagined
One with all the little
multitudes that fill the world:
ants and aphids, pollen,
bees, nectar, birds?
(The flycatcher perches on the loggia
that carries the wisteria, its blooms
now shrunken to dry, papery
fragments, each with a dot
of purple still at its center,
then swoops to collect
some little flying morsel.)
Or we could dig deeper:
the swarm of microorganisms
that till and enrich the soil,

feeding on one another
and the earth. The Many
are easier than the One.

    And so we reached toward you
through one of the little gods.
Or perhaps you reached toward us.
Who can ever tell
how a friendship began?
Who first saw whom and loved?
Whose glance was the one returned
and whose the returning eye?
Was the admiration and delight
a gift or rather the answer
to a gift? How could we know,
so early on, what treasures
would emerge in time?

    You were a two-bit desert
god, crashing through
arid mountains on your chariot
of storm, your thunder shattering
what your lightning did not burn
and torrents of water filling
the gulches and drowning whatever
could not escape. But then,
the aftermath: the flush of green,
seeds that had lain in wait
for water, grass for gazelles,
fat flies for lizards.
We knew we could not tame you.

But you invited love,
the love awakened by cool shadows
in hot places, flowing water
amid barren stones,
the ribbon of green clinging
to the streambed in dry lands.
    You cannot be surprised if we thought
you angry, given the lightning
and the flood. It would be a while
before we learned your surest,
most revealing voice
is found in stillness.

V

A Riddle for a Name

But so many voices!
One who speaks everywhere
is hard to hear. How
to distinguish tone from tone
among the unremitting
stream of sounds? Sometimes,
perhaps, we hear not yours,
but another voice, one
that means us no good.
Sometimes we hear all wrong;
the ear, perverted by the heart,
turns "fill" to "kill," turns
"love" to "slave." Your showing
of yourself, however clear,
however vivid, however
sharply delineated, always
falls at length into our meager
yet tenaciously selfish grasp,
there to be transformed
into the god we want.
        Where, then, to begin?
You reached out to attract

our notice and to claim
our love. So the conversation
begins, you trying
to speak our language,
to say in it things that couldn't
yet be said, we learning
to set your language
into our own, experimenting
with words and images, failing,
succeeding, perverting, purifying,
perfecting the words of truth,
as we suppose, only to discover
that we have locked you out
by locking our words in.

      The purest grasp of your word
is often the clumsy beginning,
still full of due uncertainty,
still baffled, still thrown off balance
by encountering you, the One.
There was Moses in the desert,
raised a prince and taught
the ways of court, washed
in the abundant waters of the Nile,
on which he'd been set afloat
to meet his fate. He learned
his dual heritage and rent it
apart in an act of violence.
And now he lives in the country
of strangers, stranger still

in its water, not given from above,
the great stream bearing it down
from distant mountains, but pulled up
by human sweat from below.
Instead of the rituals of court
and its essential gossip,
now he learns to tell
good pasturage from poisonous.
He knows the rites of mating
sheep and goats. His days
are full of predictable things
that his profession tells him
how to master. Even the
unpredictables are of a
finite number and quickly
recognized.
      And then
the bush burns and yet
it is not burnt. At first,
he thinks it one more foreign
phenomenon, albeit rare,
of this foreign land and goes
to look more closely. The voice
warns him to remove his shoes.
That alone was enough to call
a place of worship into being.
But you wanted more. You gave
him your riddle-name: "I am
what I am/I will be who

I will be/I cause what I cause."
Warning enough against trying
to pin you down! And so
you sent him off to do
the impossible, save the slaves,
lead the unwilling, make
a people. When he complained
and wanted proof, you said,
"I'll tell you what. Once
you've done it, you'll come back here
to worship."
          And this is how
you leave us, for ever trying
to grasp certainty and for ever
coming up short of the whole.

VI

Slay both man and woman, infant and suckling

Become engaged and yet
remain aloof. It seems
a good plan. Did it work?
Not at the first. We made you
more ours than you may have meant to be.
You made us in your image,
the story says. And we
have made you in ours, shaping you
as the mirror of our own
hatred and fear and wrath.
How else could it be? Could you
save a people in slavery
and not strike their masters?
Could you love your friends
without hating their enemies?
Not in that world. Perhaps
not in ours. We will not
let you.

In fairness, let's assume
that it was not Gandhi's hour,
that liberation without bloodshed
was impossible. And the army that drowned
in the Red Sea knew its risks.
Still, for every arrogant,
slave-holding commander
there were scores of peasant
recruits, hoping mostly
to live long enough
that they could go home one day
and live in a little house
with a grapevine on the arbor, a shapely
wife with large dark eyes,
and, yes, some children—perhaps one
would be a bright boy and become
a scribe and do credit to the household.
All those hopes strangled
in the returning waters.

It's easy to blame the soldiers.
We do it still. Even easier
to blame the government.
But it was you, we're told,
that set it all in motion.
From there, Canaan and genocide
were just a forty-year hop away.

Why did we think you hated them?
wanted to wipe them out?
Leviticus tells us they

were appalling, filthy people
and deserved what they got.
All those people slaughtered
at Jericho and the other cities
were just human trash, waiting
to be swept into the dumpster of history.
You'd never know they were
ever here. It's our land now.

    All this we laid to your charge,
thinking we did you honor.
We are your friends;
them you must therefore hate.
Did you, then, give the command
to kill? Can you take so lightly
the loss of those you fashioned?
No act of creation
springs from hatred. You loved them,
or you would not have molded
Canaanites out of earth's dust
with the rest of us.

        But this is useless.
Whether you commanded the deaths
or whether you merely shaped us,
the killers, perhaps it's all one.
But where is the new green
to follow the desert storm,
this storm that is all wind
and lightning and destruction?
Must we wait for ever?

However much you hoped
to stay removed, to veil
yourself behind a riddle,
you find yourself entangled
with all our worst. How
do you like that? What
will you do?

VII

God planted a garden

You wanted to make friends.
Not slaves, not subjects, not robots,
not automata to sing
your praises through eternity.
You wanted to make friends.
The mere being of all things is itself
praise enough. If that
were all you wanted, it was yours.
You chose, instead, to step back,
to throw the uncertain mix
of chance and freedom into the pot.
Did you even know, with certainty,
what sort of universe would explode
out of your beaker?
   Stone
praises you, in its low tones,
as well as angels with their high,
fluent, unfading melismas.
But if you wanted friends,
there had to be room for "yes."
And the space for "yes" is also
the room, the stage, the podium,

the reviewing stand where "no"
is spoken. Do you get more "yeses"
or "noes"? I would guess "noes."
Perhaps that's where all the missing
antimatter of the universe has gone,
burned up in our repeated
refusals of friendship.
                    You loved
the Garden, didn't you?
We loved it, too, in our own
wavering, uncertain fashion.
We are finite, after all.
We never quite know where
we are or who. We do,
however, know regret
for what is lost: the simplicity
of infant and mother, perfectly
connected by breast and mouth
and eye; the uncomplicated joy
of a perfect spring morning,
cool and warm at the same time,
crocuses with fire in their purple
chalices and a pure, faint
green spreading along the branches.
    But you don't miss the Garden.
Where you are, the Garden
always is. You miss
the quiet evening stroll,
the meeting with old friends,

the sharing of the day's events,
all made important by the love
of each for other.
                    That's
what we destroyed in grasping
for control, seeking not love
but power. We flung ourselves
into a world of force
and counterforce, of measurements
and lack, who's up? who's down?
a world not friendly to friendship,
a world of masters and slaves.

    You saw and gave it voice:
"The snake will bite your heel,
and you will stomp its head.
And you will slave for one another."

    And you waited—waited
through sweat and misery and murder
and loud threats of eternal vengeance,
waited for an Enoch who could find
in the regret for Eden a hope
for here and now. Again
you had a friend to walk with
in the green and flowering dusk,
the two of you arm in arm,
laughing over the tangled history
that brought you to this point,
happy in one another.

VIII

Let them praise his Name in the dance

What a complicated dance
it's been! First, the long
retreat, making room
on the dancefloor for the other.
Then the creative Word,
the burst of song, the clapping
of hands, immense or minuscule,
inaudible to us, but setting
the universe ahum with energy.
And, after the long and patient
waiting, the gesture of invitation—
subtle, not to frighten
the desired partner, and yet
urgent, embodying hope
so long delayed.
       Our part,
once we awaken to the music
and glimpse the extended hand,
is no less complex. We hope.
We fear. We grasp the hand.

We run away. We love.
Our love becomes a monster
of one sort then another,
outdoing all the ancient tales
of nymphs becoming trees
and weeping mothers crags.

It's not all bad, of course.
Half the delight of love
is the complex negotiation of it.
I give. You take. You answer.
Perhaps I refuse. You persist.
I'm won. But are you sure?
How does it happen? From
this dance arises a bond,
woven of many fibers,
strong enough to remake
our lives, indeed our selves.

Your tact and delicacy are things
of wonder, eliciting from atoms
dust, from dust a world
of plants and animals, from them
this human species that *might*
respond to your gesture of welcome
and join the dance of friendship.

Still more I stand in awe
of your patience, impossible to comprehend
for a mortal creature. We think
you must either put your finger
in every pie, in every

stage of every process, tweaking
here, correcting there,
working the odd miracle
for your particular favorites—
or else go away altogether,
take a long holiday, and leave
your work to its own devices.

Epicurus thought the gods
must be supremely happy.
Since no one involved in the affairs
of mortals could be so, the gods
must not trouble themselves
with the likes of us. It's plausible.

Is the alternative, then,
to see your hand everywhere,
saving the pious from sickness
or the bankruptcy court,
punishing those other folk
with lightning and flood, famine
and hail and earthquake and tsunami
and serve them right!?

Neither explains what we keep
discovering: you do not compel,
but you keep offering the hand.

IX

I do set my bow in the cloud

But about the wicked,
about our enemies—
you surely hate them.
You love righteousness.
You hate iniquity.
We don't plead some special
privilege, only that you wield
the sword of justice where it's due,
which wouldn't be on us.

And yet, I admit it's seldom
the saints among us egging you on.
It's the rest of us, the mixed lot
riding the saints' coattails
and feeling good about ourselves.
How many of us perished in the Flood,
seized by the currents and tumbled
along with the grasping, the violent,
the betrayers, the slavers, the usurers?
Our sins were petty, as were
our virtues. None of it
came to much. We authored
one another's petty annoyances

at the office, grated on the nerves
of family and friends, deserved
no great good, doubtless, but not this—
our bodies joining the flotsam
of innocent animals and trees
as the declining waters ebbed
into the sea.
         And the ones you saved?
Perhaps no better than the rest.
Noah, husband to an anonymous
wife, inventor of wine
(to his credit) and of drunkenness (not);
the sons, their wives equally
nameless, quickly turning
to dynastic politics. Ham
mocked their father the drunk;
the other two seized the advantage,
concealing his nakedness from view
with a flourish of filial piety.

   So we tell stories of your justice
or revenge and compliment ourselves
for being yet alive.
You, for your part, keep on
talking of love instead.
You set your bow in the sky
to remind you: no more
the Deluge, no more the erasure
of clumsy humanity, mixed
of good and evil, from the earth.

And still we pray, "Erase *them*!
They're the evil.
We? Well, we're not perfect.
But we're not like them."
We can't conceive—or perhaps
the saints do, but not the rest of us—
how you love, how you long over them
as over us, while we
only perpetuate the brothers'
vicious contest for preeminence.

X

Pots and Potter

We are little pots,
even the grandest, most magnificent of us.
We can't contain the downpour
of your love. And the overflow, puddling
on the ground about us, mingles
with our own senseless tears
of greed and loss and need.

And the downpour of woe?
That is still worse, threatening
to choke us with grief, the terrible
wail of infants rising
in our throats, trapped as we are
in the sorrow of the now, no memory
of yesterday's, no hope of tomorrow's
good.

We long to escape
this potdom into infinity,
the boundlessness we dream will give us
freedom and the satisfaction of our wants.
Couldn't you have created us so:
multiple infinities, never
infringed upon by others?
Or is such an infinity
only a description of Hell:

the great sinners moving
further and further apart,
avoiding all contact—unless
a few masochistic souls
follow along to serve.
(But, like every voluntary
servant, they will serve
on their own terms, to their own
purposes.) No good! The alternative
to finitude, for us if not
for you, is isolation, boredom.
How quickly little pots
fill with that! And how poisonous
it turns, fermenting and clotting
in our bowls.
          The potter makes
the vessel to some purpose—to use,
to sell, to show skill,
to inspire admiration ... to destroy?
No, here the analogy fails.
Your clay our finitude, your wheel
the turning of time, your work
of art not pots, but a multitude
of artists. Are you indifferent to your own glory?
Why invite us into being,
surrendering your own boundlessness,
making space for other hands
at the wheel, for apprentices in your art,
for associates, for friends?

XI

Leaving the Garden

And the Lord God planted a garden
eastward in Eden; and there
he put the man whom he had formed.

The garden where you first placed us—
I know it. I've spent time there—
minutes that open out on hours,
days, years, eternity.
The first peas of spring, crisp
in their unmarred greenness;
the peachtrees, a rosy celebration
hovering over all else;
hydrangeas, opening, spreading,
finding their true colors.
The mind catches on these
like sheep's wool on thorns that hold us
only to drop us back
for a moment into the dawntime.
      But we don't stay, and we didn't.
We had so little to do there
except be happy, puttering
among the plants, playing

with pet animals—nothing
to work toward beyond
the collecting of this day's dinner.
Nothing of which we might say,
"This we did, we created."

What decided us to run away?
So many things: the irrepressible
desire to leave a mark,
jealousy of your creative
edge, ambition to become
your equals, the thirst
to know, to experience, to become
wiser and more complex.
Buried in all that confusion
of purpose even lay, I think,
some longing to have a gift
to bring you in return for yours.
Did you not yourself plant in us
the desire to be friends? And what
did we have to bring to friendship?

But now we long to return
at least for a moment to the old
and un-self-conscious happiness.
No more maneuvering,
no gauging who's up, who's down;
just resting with contentment
on your chest in the woodland shade,
the fragrance of jasmine or carnation
drifting in and out

on the cooling breeze, secure
in one another's love.

Come, my beloved,
let us go forth into the field;
let us lodge in the villages;
let us see if the vine flourish,
whether the tender grape appear,
and the pomegranates bud forth:
there will I give thee my loves.

    Eden is not dead.
It is everywhere in hiding.
On a chill winter day, the wind
blustering, the rain intermittent,
tall, forked flames rise up
from the vicious aloe in the garden,
echoing the orange-red flames
of their summer counterpart, the gladiolus,
erasing time between.
Or a gray June morning of fog,
and the electric red of a pelargonium
threatens to become the nucleus
of a new creation, so compressed
and intense it must surely explode
into a new universe
at any moment.
         This time
is the dawntime. This world,

the one we share with one another
and with you, is crowded
with its possibility and memory.
Were we wrong to make
the mortal choice? Or was the fall
our doorway into a world
deeper and richer, even as
it is harsher and more threatening?

XII

Still Pursued by You

. . . and he placed at the east of the garden of Eden
Cherubims, and a flaming sword
which turned every way,
to keep the way of the tree of life.

Barred door or not,
you followed us in our flight,
never far from us.
No more the casual meeting
of old friends, strolling the garden
at dusk. We had rejected
the simplicity of that perfection.
Rather, the chance encounter
with a face familiar, but not quite
recognized, a face that inspires
longing—but for what we do not know.
There was no telling where
or when you would return.
But we built monuments to the sensed presence
and made pilgrimage to them
in hope of another meeting.
We met you at the springs and built

shrines to the nymphs, in oak groves
where we heard you whispering in the leaves,
on hilltops where we watched the skies
for signs. We met you in the songs
of poets, who could never account
for their words except by appealing
to your inspiration. We met you
in philosophers with fixed gaze, seeking
to unravel the mysteries of the One
and of the many.

          We approached with rites,
with the beauty of art, with music
(perhaps closest to your heart of all).
Sometimes you came to meet us,
sometimes not—not, at least,
to our awareness. Nothing
would be simple now. The shiver
of awe before the thunderstorm
might be a sign of your power,
but told us nothing more.

    Elijah, the righteous, the angry,
the punitive, happy to die
of famine if only he could take
the ungodly with him—Elijah
was sure you must be in the thunder,
the whirlwind shattering the rocks,
the downpour. But finally you spoke
with the still, small voice,
a voice he had never heard,

never suspected, certainly
never used himself.
He tried to complain, but the quiet
voice was surer, clearer,
sterner than the storm. Even he
obeyed. But he never encountered
it again.
        You honor our choice
for freedom. You do not abandon
your choice for love. The goal
of your creation and our lives
must somehow encompass both.

XIII

Though You Hang Back

Am I a God at hand, saith the Lord,
and not a God afar off?

You gave us moments of presence.
We imagined you as we were able:
kind or angry, faithful
or changeable, near or far.
And we imagined you as we hoped
or feared that you might be:
the lover so bound to us
you would put up with anything,
the judge so meticulous of eye
you would punish our every infraction
tenfold.
   Is any of this
what you meant to convey?
Perhaps you were just hanging out
in the neighborhood, waiting to see
what would happen with those
you once loved or still loved.
Perhaps you were playing the scorned
lover who will not be refused.

We have a trove of messages
from you—but hard to understand
or reconcile. And, strange to tell,
we sometimes recognize the handwriting:
our own, our grandparents', some even
older than theirs and now
decipherable only by experts.
In our anxiety, we read them
over as if they'd come in today's
mail, addressed to us
individually, containing directions
for the day. Like the horoscope
in the newspaper, they sometimes ring true,
more often not.
             The problem is
we want a simple account,
a single image of you,
and you evade our efforts.
As you must. Every effort
to codify you is premature. The lover
one knows at first meeting is only
a hint of the lover one knows
after two years or ten.

You are the One whose name
is simply "I am." Our name is
"We are learning." You may be
ever one and the same,
but we cannot know you so.
The "I am" only reminds us

not to take our guesses
as full or final truth.

    And yet, what a risk
you took in following us
through the gate! You left
the angel and the fiery sword
there to keep us out,
but you refused to stay behind,
safe in your walled community
from all the violence and sorrow
you foresaw. Stepping out
to accompany us, even when you
hung back and kept out of sight,
you adapted your life to ours.
Seeking friendship, you risked
change. Seeking love,
you courted us down all
our byways and detours, a God
afar off become near.

XIV

Friends of God

Who did Abram think
spoke to him, telling him
to leave country and kindred
and his father's house? And why
did he go? As a child, I never
thought it strange. How many
steps would you go back
in my family line to find
two generations living
in the same place? More than I can tell.
But Abram, we're told, was already
old and settled long
in Haran, though it was not
the land of his birth. Why
did he go? He didn't know
who you were, this voice
that called him. You promised him great things,
but promises are cheap. Why
did he go?
　　　　He fell in love.
With your voice! Foolish man
and wise. He grasped his one,

crazy moment of clarity
and moved his tents, his flocks,
his family, his slaves to a place
as foreign to him as Mongolia
would be to me.

           He'd found
a friend, whose name he did not know.
Later ages would call
the voice "the God of Abraham."
Later still you gave
your riddling name to Moses.
But Abram had only your voice.

    Abram felt free to complain,
as friends must, when the promises
were slow to be fulfilled. But still
he stayed loyal, even in the face
of famine, migration, war,
the hostility of the locals,
the strife within his family.
Sarai and Hagar vied
for precedence. Ishmael and Isaac
contested legitimacy of descent.
The children of one told the story
this way, the others that.

    You claimed him as friend.
Can children inherit friendship? Or must we make
our own, again and again?
Drawn by the voice of love,
we set uncertain feet

on the journey to the unknown land,
the place we will find ourselves
truly at home. In Mamre,
under the oaks, we shall sit,
their canopy kept green by roots
deep in the ground—there
we shall sit and talk contentedly
with our friend, sharing bread
and wine and the peace of evening.

XV

He breaketh the bow and knappeth the spear in sunder

Our words cannot contain you.
They are, at once, too fragile
and too powerful. With a word, the world
changes: becomes new with possibility
or is doomed to hatred,
pain, and destruction. No one
can say which it will be.
We are not masters of our weapons.
They break and the sherds drive deep
into our own arteries. Hitler
prophesied war, not knowing
the doom would be his own.
The sacrifice of all those others,
in widening circles of death,
in superhuman exercises of cruelty—
oh human in their arrogance—
where did it lead? Perhaps
he thought at least to build
a pyre for his own apotheosis.
But he died in a mole run.

Jupiter
was wiser. Meaning to destroy
humanity for its wildness and its violence,
he drew his thunderbolt from the quiver,
but remembered the prophecy that the aether
would catch fire and the whole world burn.
Such weapons are words.

Our words cannot contain you,
only invite—invite you to the sharing
of friendship, as you have invited us.
We risk all on a word,
knowing its fallibility, its uncertainty.
We open the mouth in hope,
turning toward the friend-to-be.
We make ourselves friends in the speaking.
The conversion is not completed
at the first turning, but there
lies the foundation of what is to come.
The words, not weapons now,
become doors by which souls come and go.

Our words cannot contain you.
It's hard to surrender the fantasy:
to know the ultimate truth
and, knowing that we know, impose it
on the rest, the fools, the heretics,
the smart alecks, the simpletons, the godless,
the misguided, the wicked, the muddled,
the arrogant—yes, especially the arrogant.
All that must go.

      Only
at dusk, beside the oaks, quiet
and at ease with one another—
another kind of word
that does not contain but conveys,
the Word of creative power,
giving birth to hope.

XVI

The Gift, the Sacrifice

Abram understood you.
Abram misunderstood you.
Friends, he thought, share
what is most precious to them.
He did not know this meant
himself, his life, his love.
He thought it meant his son.

What could you say? A friend
does not refuse the gifts of a friend.
You said, "Bring the boy
and come to Mount Moriah."
And so they came, leaving
the ass and the hired men
at the foot of the mountain, climbing
upward, the boy carrying
the wood, Abram the knife
and the blazing torch to touch
the pyre into flame, to send
the gift up to the heavens
to his beloved.
                Only one moment
before the fatal movement

did your angel intervene
to say, "No! Take the ram,
its horns caught in the thicket,
the one behind you that you never saw
in your obsession with your purposed gift.
Take this as sacrifice that isn't even yours,
and learn that you are yourself the gift I want.
All that is is mine. I created all.
I share it with you gladly. The one
gift I cannot command
is your heart."
                    Abram understood.
The ram became communion
for the three of them there. For surely
the text is wrong to say
he made it a burnt offering.
It was a peace offering and a meal
to share—a feast of tears
and reconciliation.
They ate and they were satisfied
and thanked each the other
and wept again.
      The simplicity of what you ask
of us, we cannot comprehend.
It seems too easy and it is,
in fact, too hard. How can we
esteem ourselves a gift
worthy of your greatness? How can we
imagine you ready to leave

your throne of glory, lay aside
your robes of majesty and your crown,
to embrace any one of us—Who dares
say "me"?—in the quiet garden,
under the laden fruit trees,
sharing a peach whose skin
is touched with fire and a glass
filled with the finest wine?
We would rather play hero
and wreath ourselves in glory—
however tawdry a knock-off
of yours—and fantasize that we're
desirable now. And we still
withhold what you truly desire.

  Anyway, we can find other gods
less picky and single-minded. They
won't refuse to accept our sacrifices.
The Fatherland will drink our children's
blood with equanimity. The Motherland
also. And we never lack
for high principles to justify
the bloodshed. And you weep. And we weep—
not together, not in communion,
but in mutual incomprehension.

XVII

Your Choice of Friends

Your choice of friends is broad
and (may we say?) unpredictable.
What did you see in Jacob?
Esau was bluff, hearty,
a man's man—overconfident,
to be sure—even a minute
or two of seniority can grant
a certain status. Jacob's
only accomplishments were to cheat
his brother (with Esau's rash
cooperation, yes) and deceive
his father. Piety suggests
you should have judged the scamp
and left him to stew in his guilt
till he repented. Instead,
you showed him by night the ladder
to your throne.
   The kid had talent,
not a doubt. Maybe you wanted
to see if a little adversity
might do him good, bring out
some hidden qualities, even

a sense of responsibility. It would never be
a friendship like that with Abraham.
He was a soulmate. Jacob
was all business, all schemes;
reflection was what he did when he had to.
But he could be shaken by a vision
of power beyond any he could hope for.
And he could wrestle with you,
struggling for your blessing, which otherwise
he would scarcely have noticed, would have
credited to his own cleverness.

    Esau, meantime, grew up
and became a man. He prospered.
Breezy rashness matured
to generosity. They met years later,
improbably, as friends.
And Esau ran to meet him,
and embraced him, and fell on his neck,
and kissed him: and they wept.
Were you friend to both?
Their descendants denied it as a point
of honor, not understanding your taste
in friends, not wanting to share
any good with one another.

    We still want you to ourselves.
Sometimes we go to war to prove
that you are ours alone,
that we are your only friends,
that you hate all the rest.

We put it in your mouth:
"Jacob have I loved,
but Esau have I hated."
The event disproved the charge.
If we want to credit anything
to you in their convoluted story,
let it be their meeting in peace.

XVIII

You Were in Love

Of course you were in love with David.
Who wasn't? And he drank it in
as his due. His first wife, Michal,
came to hate him for it,
could not love one who accepted
the love of all, who danced
naked before the crowds and reveled in it.
Abigail did better, having first
been married to a fool. She claimed
her portion in him and stayed
centered in her own world, the two
of them friends as well as spouses.
Saul loved him and hated him for it.
Jonathan loved him, even though
he knew he would take his place
as king.

      The ruddy, grinning
shepherd boy stayed beautiful
longer than he had any right,
despite the years of conflict,
hiding out among the Philistines,
evading Saul's spear, extorting
enough to feed his troops.

He changed from boyhood's beauty
to young man's to the deeper beauty
of the man grown full, tempered
by loss and victory and knowing
that neither is final. He grew feeble
only late in life, after Absalom,
the son he loved, tried to kill him
and take his place.
        But David,
beauty aside, seems
no likelier a choice of friend
than Jacob. He was game and steady
of nerve when taking aim
at the lion, the bear, the giant
heavily armed Goliath.
He was not pious, breaking
all the rules when he took
the holy bread to feed his men.
He saved his life by extortion,
subterfuge, betrayal. Once he was king,
he still knew how to get what he wanted:
Bathsheba, the wife of Uriah,
whom he sent to death
while she bore David's child.
Only Joab knew the truth,
Joab who did the dirty work.
Whose friend was he? Maybe
no one's, not even his own.
Joab knew—and Nathan,

but only because you told him
and sent him to prophesy to David,
to tell him that at last he had crossed
the line in harming the loyal
foreigner, the mercenary, who would not sleep
in comfort while the army slept
in the field.
        Even then
you did not abandon your friend.
You waited for him to recognize
the moment of turning, when
even a charmed life, the license
accorded a beautiful child,
reaches and overruns its limits.
He had killed, by the hand of Joab,
a friend. What could he expect from you
now? We read on—only to find
that David will be enthroned
for ever through his offspring, your love
unbroken by his deepest flaws.

    You prize not just virtue,
it seems, or piety, but every beauty
you have implanted in us. You ask us
not for perfection of life—
as if we could even conceive it—
but for intimacy of love, such
that we can still turn and repent
and accept friendship anew.
And you were in love with him.

XIX

Seductive Wisdom

You seduce us everywhere in all things
created. Yours is the beauty
of the universe and the awe,
yours the serenity of days
dawning in unbroken succession,
yours the unexpected interruption
that makes all things new.
When we've settled down in our world,
you disrupt us, jerking us awake.
When we are lost and drained of hope,
yours is the thread that leads us in
and out of the Labyrinth.
                    You are called
Lady Wisdom, the shameless
seductress who spares nothing
in heaping the table, spreading
the guests' couches, laying on
lights and music and perfumes.
Surely, my cup runneth over.
Surely, your cup is utterly
intoxicating.

For Wisdom is boundless.
Once fallen into her net, no one
ever comes to the end of her captivity
or desires to.

This is how you loved
Solomon, son of David
and of Uriah's widow, so unlike
his father that his name echoes
peace. A frightened youth,
seated on the throne by the counsel
of his mother in a palace coup,
he had nothing more than a glimpse
of your seductive beauty, of your unfathomable
depth, to draw him onward.
And even so he was wise enough
to ask for more. His thirst
was his strength. His seeking mind
was his beauty.

His songs celebrated
your love affair, the two of you
meeting and parting, seeking
and hiding, entering at last
the banqueting house. *Who is this*
that looks forth like the dawn?
fair as the moon, bright
as the sun, terrible as an army
with banners? It was you.

And when he grew old, knowing
the world would not fulfill its promises,

he returned to the simplest of things:
to eat with enjoyment, to drink
with a merry heart, to live
with one's beloved, to honor joy
as one can.
           And from youth
to old age, a life of pursuing you,
the seducer, down the turning
byways, glimpsing, losing,
finding again, peering
into every corner of the world,
led on by your inventive courtship.

XX

To Know as
We Are Known

Still, we haven't forgotten the God
we met long ago in the desert.
As Storm, battering our hearts, you evoked
the certainty of fear. And certainty
became a drug, craved
all the more when it threatened to abandon us,
while Wisdom seems fickle,
unable to make up her mind,
still weighing everything in the balance
long after time for decision
has come and gone.
                    Solomon
you loved. We're not so sure.
Too much of everything. Too much
study. Too many wives, each
with her chapel for her foreign gods.
Too much waste of good money that could
have enriched our households instead.
It's embarrassing that the apex of Israel's life
should have had presiding over it

first a beautiful ruffian, then a dreamer.
We are embarrassed for you.
But we will make it good.
We have a scheme to make things certain.
We'll write it all down. The rules
will be clear. Those who resist
will be humiliated or killed or both.

Yet, the scheme never quite works.
The old stories hold their own,
bawdy, outrageous, subversive.
The inerrant rules are forced
to consort with the songs of sinners,
pure with impure. Solomon's
voice remains alive,
astonishing, caressing, questioning,
speculating. David's temple
chorus goes on singing
anything they like, praising,
complaining, cursing, hoping.

Your Spirit is well-named, as busy
and untiring as the wind, as close to us
as our breath; and we never know
if the initiative is hers or ours.
Perhaps it is both. Even she
cannot play violin on a drum.
She plays the instrument she finds.

You try to speak our language,
but you have things to say that do not fit,
do not come through at once,

are not clear to us till we become
clear to them. So you use
our words as bait, luring us
toward something greater that we
can barely image forth in language—
the conjunction of love, when we begin
to know as we're already known.

　　When we insist that the words are yours
and yours alone, that the laws
are clear and final, that the writing
was none of our doing, you smile,
knowing that we will yet
fall through the trapdoors you have set—
none cleverer than the ones
that you and Solomon rigged
together—and into your embrace.

XXI

A Voice in the Static

Your words are hard to decipher,
your voice, submerged in the static
of chattering minds and hearts,
is hard to hear—
above all, for us the pious,
trying so hard to listen!
Jesus was never more of a problem
than for us who knew God best,
who read the scriptures and taught
the rest to know their sins.
The more confidence, the more static.
Better to confess, with Solomon,
that, finally, we do not know.
Confessing our ignorance, we make room
for friendship, we affirm beyond our understanding.

    When Jesus brought good news,
he said, "Turn and believe."
What does it take to believe
good news? Turning away from despair,
from fear and foreboding, surrender
of self-confidence, the opening of the hand
to receive goodness, the triumph
of thanksgiving over dread.

Grace

can only come as surprise.
And when grace comes, it confuses
all our accounts. All that time
spent with the double-entry columns
of our merits and our sins—all
swept away. All that deliberation,
the slow building of confident theologies—
all shattered. Yet, not all wasted.
Lying among the fragments,
we find, like Paul, the neglected
words that could have pointed us
toward the forgotten possibility,
to a knowledge of you that admits
we do not know, to a heart
willing to accept surprise.

Turn and believe the good news.
Your good news does not amend our knowledge of you.
It upends it, till every element of it,
shaken loose in free fall,
rearrange itself to form
a picture we recognize and yet
could not have drawn before.

Turn and believe. There is no hearing
of your voice that does not transform.
And no single hearing
that transforms once and for all.
Always some static remains,
blurring the voice we hear.

Grace, even when we have known it
many times before,
will still find ways to surprise.
Its music penetrates the gabble
and we are astonished and we are changed.

XXII

Leaving Haran

The hummingbird flashing by me
on the path makes a whir
like a mechanical toy. Toy
and bird alike may bring
delight. But the toy is at someone's
beck and call. Not so the bird.

    You must have built into us
the desire to create and control—
part of the very image
you stamped on us, albeit
gone awry. You are less thirsty
for control than we. How else
could you have created this universe,
enlisting quantum uncertainties
and the slow contingencies of evolution
as your allies? You don't mind
surprises, do you? We
don't much like them.

    Hence, I suppose, the favorite flaw
of our religions. We build them to delight in you
and then rebuild them to contain you.
From birdwatcher's blind to birdcage!

We started small—with fetishes
to keep you where we needed you,
with talismans so that we had you at need.
Our skills at imprisoning you
kept pace with our cultural sophistication.
We made images you could inhabit,
temples you could not leave.
We invited you into our cities
and then bound you to protect them.
When all these failed, we endowed
religion itself with infallibility,
guaranteeing we would never be surprised,
never caught off guard by the hummingbird
that whistles past our ear without warning.

The worship called forth by your love
and power is always alloyed
with our desire to be safe from you.
What better solution than a mechanical
toy god, guaranteed always right,
guaranteed always the same,
guaranteed to respond on command
and to sit quietly till summoned
again. Put the infallibility
wherever, it is all the same:
the pontiff, the book, the consensus
of the generation past, the tradition
of elders more remote. Pay
no attention to the shrieks you may hear
from outside. It is only the groaning

of the juggernaut's great wheels
or perhaps the cry of some crushed
soul who deserved destruction.

All to protect us from surprise.
Our love for you and our fear
are seldom far apart. The wonder
of the saints—the true saints,
some of them even in the calendar—
is that, more and more, they are caught up
in the love, while the rest of us use
our piety to build ourselves a fortress
and keep your surprises out,
thinking it a jail to keep you in.

But where is the map for the perilous
journey from false saint to true?
How does an Abram leave Haran
for an uncharted future?

XXIII

Bougainvillea

The low rays of early morning sun
slide past trees and buildings
and kindle the bougainvillea into a bonfire,
its light bouncing again
off the glass doors of a workshop
still in shadow, yet now set ablaze.
        What do we need to be human?
You told us to ask for bread
for every day. And not the dry
bread of penitence—you were never
an ascetic. We ask for bread
of true substance, whose crumb
and crust bring joy as well as sustenance.
        In the desert, you gave the people
one day's manna at a time.
It made them anxious, so short
is the sight of human faith;
now you let us ask
the bread for tomorrow as well.
A little security, then—
this, too. And clothing and shelter,

enough for the place and season
and a little more for delight in ornament.

And, above all, beauty and the arts.
As well the singers as the players on instruments
shall be there: all my springs are in thee.
What are we without music?
When we began to sing we became
human—and when we began
to make necklaces of shell
and tools of stone and bone,
when we began to grind
colors and paint with them,
shape clay, cook new foods,
and pile stones up to mark
the places of your appearing. You planted
Eden. We followed your example
and have been gardeners ever since,
selecting the sweetest fruits,
fragrant and resplendent flowers,
herbs for the healer and the chef.

Hence the catching of the breath
with which we see the rays
of the reborn sun metamorphose
some vast shrub,
a dull haystack by moonlight,
into a celebration of delight, your gifts,
and the dawn of the human soul.

XXIV

Letter and Spirit

Once there were tablets written
by your own hand. Moses
smashed them before anyone could read them.
We wouldn't have understood them anyway—
no more than Belshazzar understood
what you wrote on his wall.
Moses expected to be Lawgiver
and grew angry to find he had
to be their teacher instead
and write the textbook, too.
The work wore him down—answering
questions, correcting mistakes,
dealing with his brother's undermining
of the work, containing the ill effects
from disasters in the lab. It was a mercy
that you showed him the Promised Land
from Nebo, but didn't let him go there.
How grim to learn that nothing
had changed after the commencement exercises!
        The second set of tablets
was written in Hebrew, a language
of our own. They, too, are lost.

And so began the thousand years
of recovery and reinvention. We wrote down
what we could remember, some of it
still fresh in our minds, some of it
verbatims of conversations from centuries before.
Like students trying to rebuild
old, half-understood lectures
from incomplete notes, we labored out
the work and we learned as much
in the task of reconstruction as from our first,
glazed hearing.
           The work was human
and divine, born of your speech
and of our struggle to hear
and fostered by your Spirit, first
brooding the egg to keep it warm,
then fanning it with storms to quench
the fevers of arrogance that threatened
to distort its growth.
           The same
Spirit speaks in us still,
questioning, pointing, seducing,
admonishing. And still she broods
our hatchling comprehension and still
she fans her immense wings
to sweep away the fogs of self-certainty,
the mortal fevers of our fanaticisms,
the deathlike rigor of the-way-it's-always-been.
When she is agent of destruction,

we find it hard to remember
that she is agent of life.

    No written word alone
can take her place. The word
becomes alive again by her gift.
And we resume the task of listening
for your voice, saying things hard
to utter in our languages and hard
to hear, saying things we can understand
only as we are transformed by them.

    Who knows the meaning of "love"
till love awaken love?
I sleep, but my heart waketh:
it is the voice of my beloved that knocketh, saying,
Open to me, my sister, my love,
my dove,
my undefiled.

XXV

Weariness

You don't seem to grow weary of us,
as we do. Sometimes, Armageddon
seems the preferable alternative.
We would like to immolate our enemies,
making a holocaust to our god
of the moment, the one that seems
to us so great, so final we can't imagine
how utterly eclipsed he'll be
in three generations and in four.
And if we do not succeed,
well, we'll throw ourselves on the pyre,
dragging as many of them as we can
in with us.
        And we'll lay it to your charge.
You must have ordered it. We heard you
speak through the mouth of Molech
or of Asshur, of Hitler or Mao,
of priest or prophet or philosopher,
of the nation or the empire or the market—
even sometimes in a voice that sounded
so very much like your own.
And the voice said, "Kill!" We're sure it did.

Or sometimes, "Enslave and kill!"
Or again, "Convert and kill.
Kill for the purity of the race.
Kill for the safety of your families.
Kill for the purity of the doctrine.
Kill for me." Surely
we heard aright; we couldn't
have mistaken; the words were plain.
    And you weeping the while.

    How do you endure the anguish?
Some say if we could dispense
with you, we'd be free of the killing.
I think if you thought it would work,
you would withdraw. But it's no good.
You couldn't take the idols with you.
They belong to us. We just
rename them and reconfigure their faces
and send the wretched to their deaths
for the glory and liberty of the market
or nation or -ism instead of you.
    Words are too stupid to express it.
There should be only tearstains on the page.
But too long familiarity leaves us
dry-eyed.
        Where are your fathomless
wells of tears that we might share them?

Therefore I will bewail with the weeping of Jazer
the vine of Sibmah:
I will water thee with my tears,
O Heshbon, and Elealeh:
for the shouting for thy summer fruits
and for thy harvest is fallen.

Why have you not grown weary of us?

XXVI

How Speak of You at All?

How can we speak of you at all
in human language? Anything
we can say misrepresents you.
Poetry is least inadequate
to the task because its weaknesses
are so palpable. It makes do with leaps
and angular glimpses and connections
that always threaten to snap
with the strain. It is shored up
with rhythm and with music and the goodwill
of the listener. Its pretenses to system
or completeness are laughable.
Its failure to capture you is its gift.

    The closest thing to your mystery
is our own. Angels are transparent
by comparison, however ancient
and rich their minds, however far
beyond ours their grasp extends.
You are deeply complex.
We know you in the storm and in the calm.
We know you in the green of opening buds
and the fires of leaf-fall and in snow.

We recognize you in the thousand gradations
of wind and breeze and gale
and in the breath that sustains, refreshing
the blood with itself. But we know you
above all in one another.

Yes, we recognized long ago
that our casual fashioning of you
in our image was just another
trick of our desperate imagination,
as one image after another
collapsed from the burden of addressing you.
Euhemerus said if horses
had gods, they would look like horses.
Quite so. If horses had gods,
they'd be in the same predicament as we
and fall back on the same device.

We know no mystery more enduring
or creative or unfathomable than our own,
but we sense one,
the author of those love notes
that keep coming to us with no
return address, who may meet us
anywhere but has no permanent
home, there always to be found.

And therefore we speak unabashedly
of you, as though one like us.
We speak of you as maker and destroyer,
as changeable of mood and purpose,
as judge and lover, as giver

of law and lavisher of grace.
Such dangerous words!
It's easy to latch onto this one
or that and forget that the whole
remains unfathomable and beyond
speech. We take our verbal scraps
and make you a mirror of our hopes
or fears, our dreams or nightmares,
even fashioning from you an excuse
for our greatest crimes.
                    And yet,
no lesser mystery will suffice,
no less dangerous image be adequate.
You are not like us, but you are never
less than we. And sometimes
we see you clearly in one another—
fleetingly, of course, and indirectly,
but something breaking through,
some light that signifies one *beyond*,
however far away across reefs
and chartless water, whom we recognize
and hope to see again.

XXVII

Your Image

Being made in your image—
it sounds like an honor, a gift,
a claim on your consideration.
It's also a lot of trouble.
How can one imitate the One?
Our temptation is to puff up as big
as possible and try to seem
important. But then we look more
like toads, all jowls and warts.
Or we aim at always being right—
never a mistake, and if there is,
keep straight on. Maybe nobody noticed.
Outface the doubters, even yourself.
Or perhaps we can expand our power
to mirror yours—missiles for thunderbolts.
And if we cannot make a green Earth,
we can at least mar one. It all turns,
too often, ugly in our hands.

Your experiment, if that's what it is,
in freedom hasn't prospered
as you must have hoped. Even
our virtues turn into vices.

Still, here and there, someone
hears and listens for a moment
and does some generous and hopeful
act, and we glimpse your image
moving across our field of vision.
Maybe we even turn our heads
to see where it might lead.

The generosity of lovers, that's
where we are at our best
and most like you, our true
original. First, the gift
of freedom, without which
no second gift, the gift
of self. The fruits of your sowing
are often hidden away
from public gaze, exchanged
in the glances of lovers, the encouragement
of friends, the placing of the best
portion on the stranger's plate.
So Abraham and Sarah received
the strangers on their way to judge
and destroy. And Abram did not
neglect to plead for the lives
even of your most arrogant
and violent creatures. If their violence
was the risk in your gift of freedom,
his plea was its glory, an act
of grace reflecting your likeness.
So one imitated the One,

even calling you to account
at the bar of your own mercy.
 Was that your purpose all along?
That some friend might know you
well enough to call you back
to yourself? Did you need that?
Were you so forgetful?
Or did you simply long for it,
long for such intimacy with us?
 Such a longing would know only
one thing, how to unfold
and replicate itself again
and again, bestowing the gift
of freedom with the gift of love.

XXVIII

Prophecy

It's hard being your prophet. For every true
there are many false, and only you
can see the difference. They themselves
may not know. Human as they are,
each is a mix of response
and resistance, driven at times
by your Spirit and at times by their own spleen
or optimism, their recklessness or their desire
to command. How are the rest of us
to tell? Whom to believe? Whom to reject?
Only the dead ones, winnowed
by history and the canon makers,
are safe and can be trusted.
And they weren't speaking to us.

    The TV prophets have become a joke,
always threatening the wicked with storm
and flood and earthquake. And when these fall,
all unexpected, on their flock, they become
a test of faith and not a punishment.
Why not admit that the pious
suffer along with the wicked?
Job was honest enough to say so.
So, too, Solomon. Why not they?

And then we have your true prophets, always
suffering disgrace for saying
what their public didn't want said.
Perhaps that's our best clue. And yet,
prophets sometimes utter peace,
can rejoice in restoration, can urge
renewal and rebuilding. There are prophets
of hope, as there are prophets
of doom and judgement.
                    Jeremiah
preached both, but mostly gloom
—and suffered richly for it,
shut out of family celebrations,
dumped down a well, near death
from starvation, forbidden to speak,
kidnapped and taken abroad
to teach him better manners.
And he complained, as well he might.
Was there ever a moment of joy?
Was your seduction so cruel
that you only used him, like Cassandra,
to speak oracles no one would believe?
Did you give him at least
one long embrace, one
melting together before
he took up his post, a love
concealed from us now
behind all the talk of war?

XXIX

Hope Is More Difficult than Fear

The words of oracles are seldom
clear, least of all
when they seem clearest.
Were those who uttered them
any more certain of their meaning
than those who heard? We
may look back through intervening years
and spot a clue here, a fulfillment
there—and, yes, also the failures,
the point where prophet or interpreter
went wrong in the details. But still
they were right about the doom.
Doom comes to every nation,
early or late, most certainly
to the most powerful, but also
to the weak who fail to notice
that the world is changing around them.
To those who said, "This is our god
and must protect us," your prophets
said, "This is God of all

and has a whole world to care for."
This was the most painful thing
they told us, that you were not ours
alone, that you, who brought us up
from Egypt, brought the Philistines
from Crete and the Arameans from Kir.
How could you love them,
if you love us? How extend
your hand to help them? How
settle them next door? How
invite them to the feast of milk
and honey?

How can your love
be limitless? We only know
love that says "No" to some
in order to say "Yes" to others.
It's all we can achieve. But you
love our enemies. You love
your enemies. You leave
no one out.

Is this the wellspring
of your hope, from which Isaiah,
second of the name, drew oracles
of restoration after everything was lost?
Oracles of good news, of rejoicing
for the barren, of returning home
for exiles, of the renewing of love
for those who had abandoned you
and thought you had abandoned us?

Such prophecy is difficult as the prophecy
of doom. Where did he find
courage to offer reassurance
in time of despair? Didn't he fear
it was all delusion, all
fantasy, that he might be sending
the exiles back, defenseless,
to crash against those who remained,
clinging to the ruins, occupying
abandoned houses—what
was left of them—struggling
to make their own new start
in what had fast become
a wilderness again, home
to jackals and owls and the ghosts
of slaughter? Could they expect
anything more than renewed
conflict?

      Generations after,
Haggai was still nerving them
to rebuild the Temple, to reclaim
their love affair with you.
Hope is more difficult than fear.
Love alone awakens it.

XXX

Gratitude

A wash of raspberry jam
across a slice of toasted
sourdough, transparent as watercolor,
dotted with flecks of darker red,
through it the complex texture
of the bread showing, the center
of the slice still white, the edges
brown, the crust darker still.
   It's hardly a rare event
in my routine that it should sit here
on my writing table, my second
cup of coffee its companion.
Both fade into the commonplace,
and then I wake up and see them
again and admire their beauty
and the intricate interweaving of your gifts
and ours (yes, also yours)
that brings them to this place
and moment.
        I'm made newly
grateful, knowing well
it was not inevitable that I

should sit at this table with my work
and this richness of sight and smell,
taste and nourishment. Born
in another place or time,
born with less quickness of thought
or fewer gifts for making
my way through the maze my world
set before me, born with a different
mix of strengths and weaknesses,
I wouldn't be sitting here.

    My gratitude mixes itself
with the guilt of a survivor. I wonder
if I am one of those rich that Amos
denounced for battening off the poor.
I suppose I am. How does anyone
live in the tangle of our times
without being part of the web
of unequal exchange?

           The Marxists
thought they could rid the world of it.
They only succeeded in transforming
one currency of inequality into another.
There is, it seems, no magic bullet
we can fire into the monster's brain.
There's only the slow slog of conscience
and generosity. Blessed is the people
that has them for its guide, that can restrain
the forces of market and government,
of local dictators and global

conglomerates, and look to the needs
of the weak, the sharecropper, the cast-off
child, the wounded, the broken.

   There is still need, then,
for gratitude, for delight at raspberry
jam on toasted sourdough
with the aroma of coffee.
The sharing of delight multiplies
delight. Gratitude implies
obligation. You didn't mean
these goods for me alone.
The starving, too, you love.
And what good is it to them,
if ingratitude makes us selfish?
Your quest for friendship costs you
pain for every moment
of fulfillment, every delight
of love—deep loss for everyone
shoved aside on the way.

XXXI

Balaam and the Ass

You told Balaam to go
and not to go—first no,
then yes, then no, then yes
again. At length, you sent him
to tell the king the very things
he didn't want to hear.
He'd have liked to prophesy
as Balak wished and have the agreed
reward. But to his credit he held firm.
To be sure, the lecture he had
from his faithful ass and the sight
of the towering angel, blocking
the road with drawn sword, helped
impress on him the gravity of the situation.

But prophets are as vulnerable to temptation
as anyone—as vulnerable as priests
and pastors, as monks and nuns,
as prelates and popes and deacons
and all the faithful of whatever stripe.
It always seems easier to comply
and speak the desired lie
to power, to anoint the slogans

of the regime, the war that they've
determined on, the repression of their foes.

    Balaam had a living to make,
like the rest of us. He could have retired
on what Balak was offering him.
But then where would he go?
The uppity ass would probably
refuse to carry him.
His servants, who'd already
seen him lose one argument
to her, would laugh at him
behind their sleeves. And the angel
might not sheathe the sword
next time.

       Too bad for the rest of us.
Our dangers are less obvious and compelling
than Balaam's angel. And conscience
is easier to silence when it's only
a voice inside our heads.
Let it speak through the mouth of an ass
and perhaps we would take notice.

XXXII

Piety

As if self-interest and self-obsession
were not enough, as if lassitude
and distraction didn't suffice
to keep us from you, our most dangerous
temptation is our pious fervor.
We hope to commend ourselves
to you, setting ourselves apart
from the herd of bleating sheep
who only follow you for the pasturage
and the still pools of water.
And then they wander off and lose themselves
in the rocks, get caught halfway
up absurd, cliff-hanging ledges,
eat things that make them sick,
fall prey to lions and wild dogs.
        Fear not! We'll keep them
in line for you, set them
a good example, harry them
when they stray again, invoke
your wrath and punish as needed.
If nothing helps, then cast
the wicked into outer darkness

so that the timid will remember
to obey.
        Elijah was your friend
and ready to defend you to the death,
his own or anyone's. How many
corpses did he account for?
Four hundred fifty prophets
of Baal, four hundred of Asherah.
But no one knows the toll
of drought and famine, the diseases
that carried off the starving,
the malnutrition that never loosed its hold
even on the survivors. So much
for the people. There were also
the animals, collapsed around
the dry springs, and the pasture grasses,
eaten down to the roots—all dear
to you as their maker, all dead.
And this he did to honor you.
Jonah was another in that mold.
He would not preach to Nineveh
for fear the evil would repent
and you would forgive. Both of them
loved you—but not so much
as they loved their own righteousness.
Had they loved you more,
they'd have learned your loves
and come to share them.

            Can the pious
ever become lovers? Can we give
enough, surrender, risk
enough, to see you as you are
and catch the abundance of your love
and share it? Can we admit
you love the common herd
as much as us? even the stray
you have to ferret out
from among the rocks and thorns
because of its stupidity or ours?
      Forgive our piety. Teach us
to see, as Jonah could not,
its cruelty. Rescue us, if you can,
from this wilderness of thorns
we have made or wandered into,
thinking we were on the path
to grass and water, stupid
sheep that we seem to be.

XXXIII

Seeking Friends

How many times have you drawn near
to one person here, another there,
seeking friends? Your Word
has spoken all through history,
drawing us to observe, to reflect,
to reason. Your Spirit presses
us to look past our palisades,
to imagine things unthought,
to make beauty, to contrive art.
Your Wisdom gives discernment
and the power to turn and be renewed.
You have offered us yourself.
Sometimes we accept your offer
and walk with you some little way.

Then, if only briefly, hope
expands and courage grows.
We dare join your work of creation.
Without you, our hands are weak,
our generosity insufficient for the task.
Without us, you cannot complete
what you began, cannot arrive
at the consummation, the banquet on the mountain,

the ingathering from near and far
into the Holy City, the healing
of wounds, the bridal chamber.

When you made us, you sacrificed
your blessed solitude. Alone,
you were never lonely. Now
you know how to feel loss.
Unless you can draw us into the parks
by the River of Living Water,
the sweet meadows, sprinkled
with wildflowers and bordered by trees
whose fruit fails not and whose leaves
heal the nations, unless
you can persuade us to live there in peace
with you and with one another,
you will be alone indeed,
bereft of the love you lavished on us,
no return for the ardent
glance you cast on us.

Do not give up on us! Slow
though we are, we may not be
finally obdurate. Love
can still waken hope, and hope
give rise to trust, and trust
may yet deliver us into your embrace.

XXXIV

Love

The church has been nursery of anger,
piety its finishing school.
We who think ourselves worthy
are always ready to point out
the others: the slackers, the heretics.
We dream our own perfection. We endow
ourselves with too much authority.
We mistake high office for godliness,
the excess of denial for holiness.

You gave us one sure direction:
Love one another, for love is of God.
And we've found a thousand ways around that.

Perhaps we should overthrow
the whole absurd construction.
Away with hierarchs, away
with visible pieties, let everything
be inward, personal, pure.
But then holiness becomes nameless,
inarticulate, private, secret.
For the public realm there is left
only a vague longing,
easy prey for the next fanaticism.

There's no escaping the mix
of good and evil in things human.
Church is not immune.
Unchurch is not immune.
For every Francis there will always be a score
of inquisitors usurping his name,
for every inquisitor ten commissars
protecting political purity.
Still, there *was* a Francis.
Someone heard the promise
and gave consent to it
and burst into flames of love.

The church is a nursery of anger
and a nursery of love and a ring
where the two are for ever
joined in a wrestling match
for our hearts. Religion's
trappings do not save,
nor the piety of those who spend
long days in prayer and fasting.
It is the love hidden in the crevices,
flashing out when least expected,
sometimes suppressed, always
fought against, yet never
vanquished. Here we recover
the true center—and see
that we have known it all along.
You put a taste of it on our tongue
at the creation so we might recognize it again.

For love you made the world
and us in it. For love you have drawn us
with Word and Wisdom, transformed us
with Spirit. For love you have searched
us out and known us—and made known
the costliness of your desire for us,
the pouring out of your own life.

XXXV

Hands

In the garden, we walked the swept path
in the heat of late afternoon, the rays
of the low sun filtering
through a row of ancient cypresses.
A bench there, older than the trees,
looks out over slopes covered
with ruins, broken too long
to cause sorrow now,
only wonder that this much beauty
can survive our penchant for desolation.

    What are we doing here,
seated on this bench, our
hands entwined, the first breath
of evening brushing against us?
How does this gesture, so familiar,
seem fresh and unexpected?
Whence does love have the power
to renew itself again and again?

    Face to face with time's
passing, civilizations in decay,
the finite, bounded, dumb
facticity of everything, we rediscover

love. It must be more fragile
than these broken buildings,
more than the people who lived
and died here and are no more.
Yet, it reasserts itself.
We rediscover it, hand in hand.
     This is how we persist.
We don't give up on one another.
We don't give up on ourselves.
We live by the gift of the past,
even on the lip of the ruins.
This bench, left by some ancient
benefactor who looked out from it
on a busy city below,
offers an unintended prospect now,
but it remains a gift. This path
someone laid out long ago,
this morning someone else
has swept. We have walked on gifts
and seated ourselves on gifts.
     If, for the moment, our attention,
focused between us on hands
linked and linking, withdraws
from the ruins, the past, the inheritance
of others' loves, they are not lost.
We are made by them,
we ourselves the next
link of chain, the next
loop of fabric on the loom,

the synapse of communication between
past and future. Nothing
but love can give this gift.

    You committed it to our care
from the beginning, making us
by your love, then seeking us
by your love. You met us
in the garden then, as you do now.
You sit with us on the bench
that looks out over everything,
all past, all future, all worlds.
This is the center of all that is.
This is the home of the One who is.
There is no greater than Love.

    And you invite us together here,
to sit with hands entwined
in the shade of cypresses, far above
the ruins with their lingering beauties,
absorbed in one another and in you.

XXXVI

Capturing the Light

You spoke and there was light,
your first great gift to us,
the flinging back of shutters,
day driving the shadows before it.
After the gasp of awe,
our first thought
was how to steal it for ourselves.

It was your opening move in the game—
to flood the board with light.
We quickly learned to skulk
under the table, hiding
aces, trading marked cards,
trying to figure out your trick
so we could do it, too.

But your self-revelation was the trick,
wasn't it? It's hard to do that
in the dark, out of sight.
It needed a big stage and a lot
of daring. You made your own light
out of the transparency of your word.
And you shared it with us as a gift.
And, try as we may, we can't figure out

how to reduce it to a possession,
how to direct it where we like,
keeping it off our underhanded dealings,
keeping it under our secure control.

    And this was just the beginning.
Suspicious and uncomprehending though we are,
you kept reaching out, seeking friendship.
You compromised yourself by keeping company
with the likes of us. You opened yourself
to blame for our misdeeds. And then,
you stood among us as human as we—
your word, your light, now become flesh,
exposed to all our vicissitudes,
vulnerable, like us, to fear and failure.

    At last, the light in a form we could grasp!
You made it easy. You didn't run.
We caught you, one way and another.
Some caught hold of your flesh and said,
"At last, we'll be rid of this one;
the gifts will be ours alone."
Some caught fire from your sun
and became your friends. Most of us
wavered and waver still,
unable to decide: friend
or foe?

      You didn't make it easy.
We couldn't get a grip on you. Even
when we weave artful bars
around you to keep you in your place

and make you, who forswore violence,
patron of our cruelty and mayhem,
you keep on preaching through the bars,
offering to heal our terrors,
to calm our panic, to renew our life.
    We cannot catch light,
only be caught, take fire from it.
The word became flesh in order to flash forth
as light again—revealing and challenging us.
We fail. But you do not.
You still make inroads into our shadows.
You still speak light into being
and throw back shutters we thought we had nailed fast.

XXXVII

Bridegroom

What drew the crowds after you in your wanderings?
Your stories made us uneasy.
Your teaching seldom comforted.
There was no fantasy, no assurance
that everything would come right.
Even the miracles were unnerving,
though we all flocked to get one
for ourselves. You raised the dead girl,
then denied it. You refused the woman
of Canaan, then gave her what she asked
and freed her daughter from the demons.
But you would do nothing without our consent.
At Nazareth, they couldn't see anything new
in their old homeboy, and you
could do nothing, could awaken in them
no sense of hope. Still
people flocked to you. Why?
In the hope of gain, of course.
Because other people were doing it.
Looking for revolution, maybe.
Mostly because they saw in you
a person strong enough to be free,
free enough to love.

You called yourself
once "the bridegroom." Desire
brought you to us and your desire
awakened ours. We wanted
to set eyes on you, even from the edges
of the crowd. We wanted to hear
your voice as much as your teaching.
We wanted to touch you. If only
the crowd would part a moment
like the Red Sea and usher us
into the future! We were Bartimaeus,
shouting and wailing by the roadside,
making such a disturbance that you would hear
and turn and call for him. You asked him
what he wanted. He said,
"My sight." You gave it and he saw—
you. And he followed as you went
to Jerusalem and the cross.
                            Is that
what he asked for? No.
He just wanted to see the world
around him, to learn a trade,
not to have to beg
anymore, maybe learn to read
for himself. But what he saw
was you. And he didn't go back
to his home in Jericho. He went
forward with his beloved into a future
completely unknown.

This is how
you brought us to you. You drew us
by cords of love, by bands
of beauty, with the hope of the bridegroom's
kiss. And the love thus sealed
bound us to you for ever.

XXXVIII

The Tree of Life

At the summit of the world stands the tree of life,
first to catch the light of creation,
first, however often benighted,
to catch the returning sun.
There we have lived from the beginning.
There we return as long as we breathe,
inhaling its freshness, renewed by its fruit,
healed by its sap and bark and leaves.

By the strength it gave, we dared
the brilliant light of the savanna
with its treasures and dangers; we set
our own stamp on the life we were given.
We dug roots and hunted game.
We made fire and built shelters from the sun.
We found trees that reminded us of home,
and we planted their seeds and shoots
and took pleasure again in their shade.

Our going out and coming in—
all is a circling round the tree
and a returning. But once we came
and found it stripped to bare wood,
outside the city, and a body

hanging from it. Was it to block
our way back for ever that we did it?
to sever our ties and shut
the gate to the garden? There have been
many, many bodies since.

    Of one it is told that the tree
returned to life. Watered
by that one's gift, it put forth
new roots, new branches; leaves
unfolded, buds became blossoms,
fruit followed. And a fragrance we had forgot,
a taste pungent and yet sweet,
a freshness in the air, a leaf
that, held to old scars, softened
and drew the anger from them—
all these things we had forgotten
met us again and gave hope.
While the tree lives, we live.

    This doesn't keep us from trying
to kill it, nor from using it to kill
others. This is how terrified
we are of the gifts, how determined
to owe no one anything, even thanks.
This is how easily we deceive ourselves,
dividing the common into private
plots, building our walls,
locking the gates, drawing
lines of power on the map,
and fighting to control them.

Still,
the tree is there, at the summit,
where you planted it at the beginning,
a seed taken from your own heart,
watered with your own lifeblood.
And it will be there at the end
when all else fails, shedding
leaves to heal the nations,
welcoming us back to its shelter.
    Do I hope too much?
Perhaps. But I choose to hope.
The love that launched us out into the sun
has never quit us. It goes with us,
whispering in the ear, waking
the imagination, applauding our inventiveness,
weeping for our wrongs, rejoicing
as we learn again to give,
to love as we are loved,
to hope that the tree lives still
and that we shall see it at the last day.

XXXIX

Your Beauty

Your beauty we cannot express.
On a calm morning of high clouds,
you are the shadowless, light-filled
space among trees. In the afternoon,
you become the shade that wasn't there
this morning, just as you are the sun
that throws it there—both heat
and coolness. You are the evening
fog that chills, sending us
indoors to warmth and food,
there meeting us again
among familiar faces
that have joined us on our journeys.
You are the seed and the shoot,
the flower, the fruit and again the seed,
the wind's music and the sound
of rain.
            I know a place
where the morning lingers
among eucalpyts and redwoods.
Nothing is heard but the stirring
of leaves in the wind and the splash

of an old fountain, left behind
from richer days. The fog
carries the fragrance of the trees.
The light is evenly diffused.
There, for a moment, everything
is everywhere, the dampness of fog
against the skin is one
with the spread of light on the eyes
and the soughing, trickling sound.
There is no there, no here,
no near, no far, but beauty
is all and gives herself
to her loved ones lavishly, without stint.
    Your beauty is beyond our power
to express. It draws us; we respond.
We never grasp it, reduce it
successfully to words. And we never stop
trying. It is our joy, our delight,
to praise what touches us with wonder
and awakens love. To rest
in love is good. To sing
love is golden. The resting
teaches us the song. The singing
returns us to rest in you.

XL

Infinity

To be finite in the presence of infinity
exalts and terrifies. The eyes
take in the vast swirl of the galaxy.
The mind struggles to understand
that it is only the least drop
of the universe. And, beyond the one universe,
others? However far off
the bounds of our perception, there remains
a beyond. To stand here
in our littleness and become witnesses
of the All, this is exaltation.
The terror is its aftershadow.
What does infinity grasp of us?
Are we beetles beneath the elephant's feet?
Are we kindling for some great conflagration?
Are we an unintended consequence
of processes that know only how to tag
one step endlessly onto another?

No wonder we have given you
so many different names,
attached so many stories
to you, devised so many ways

to bend infinity to finite wills.
If one of our religions fails,
we will try another. If that
becomes oppressive, we will have
none at all. But we are still
ants beside the ocean,
clinging to grains of sand,
trying to see over the waves,
hoping not to be swept away
by the breaking surf. Whether it be
hostile or merely indifferent,
it remains boundless and beyond control.

How can anyone think of you
as Love? How can the Infinite love
some evanescent cipher,
some mayfly, some flower that withers
in the hand that plucks it? And how
would the cipher-mayfly-flower
know itself loved?

Jesus talked such nonsense.
No one would believe him if he hadn't
also found in it strength to live
right through to death and more.
A lover seized by love,
awash in it, borne along by it,
splashing it on the rest of us
till we begin to soften with it—
only such a one
could speak such nonsense and be heard,

even believed and followed by one here,
one there, people lit
by new fire and daring to burn.
     And, yes, still little ciphers.
But instead of clinging to their grains
of sand, hoping for protection
from you, they wade into the tide
and let it carry them.
     For a moment, when the sky
is clear at dawn, the low sun
will shine between eucalyptus trunks,
touching into color what will be shadowed
the rest of the day. For that moment,
the grove reveals a splendor
unsuspected. And then it vanishes.
To frame the beauty of three
perfect minutes needs
the same love as the creation of a universe.
Your infinity makes room even
for the infinitely small, the vanishing,
the ant on the shore.

XLI

The Learning of Love

Of your goodness, you have not left us
marooned on the edge, staring
into the abyss. We spend
our moments there, and then
return to the human world.
Here we learn love, the gift
given and received; and here
we practice it, often clumsily.
Our hands produce shrill screams
on the instrument when we are careless
or uncomprehending. Sometimes we correct them.
We sense that beauty is still possible
if we can find the note.
        Or sometimes we prefer
the sense of privilege that comes
with refusal to give. Our world
becomes snarled and knotted then.
Love is a gift that only the giver
receives. Like manna in the desert,
it molders when hidden away, produces
worms and begins to stink.
Unlike money, it has no use

except to benefit the beloved
and to rejoice in the gift. Clever
invention that leads us back,
circling, to you and to ourselves!
The bliss is not in the receiving,
but in the exchange.

By love alone can finite
specks be brought to joy,
be bound to one another and to you
who were once boundless, but are so
no more. Love gives life
to the other, pays fealty
to the soul of the beloved, the distinct
and living presence, without whom
there is no exchange of love.
You limited yourself to bring us forth,
made room for us to live,
to love or not, as we
may choose.

You know that "yes"
does not come easily to the lips
of frightened beings, standing
on the edge of the infinite. And you
have become the most patient of lovers
and most faithful, drawing us out of our dead ends
to your door, inviting us in
to break our fast on fragrant
bread and your intoxicating cup.

XLII

The Twelve

A strange array you picked
to be your little crew
of deputies—all men for one,
though you had many women
with you, then as now.
Did the men require
special attention, stricter
discipline? Was the gospel
of love harder for them to grasp?
    They weren't self-selected,
would never have formed a team
on their own initiative. Peter
was always out front, falling
on his face; Simon the Zealot
standing at the edge, waiting
to catch another fault
in his less pious brethren.
Andrew and Philip were doers,
trying to get on with the business
of the day, if only they could learn
what it was. Thomas,
always perplexed. Judas

Iscariot, the one who could keep score
and therefore held the ministry
of the exchequer. Matthew, the reformed
tax-collector, never fully
trusted by the rest. As odd
an assortment as one's own family
or the people where one works.

It was a wonder anything got done.
When it did, it was you doing it.
They kept the women and children
back. You welcomed them in.
They would have sent the crowds away.
You fed them. They wanted your teaching
for themselves, so they could dole it out
to the seeking multitudes. You wasted
your best lines on the crowds. And when
they wanted to sit on thrones
in your kingdom, you said, "Sure.
But just watch first and see
how I do it—from a cross."

Men don't deal well with surrender,
even the idea of it. Win or die fighting.
They rebelled against the whole concept:
loving the enemy, dying
to expose the evil. It would take them
a lifetime to figure it out.
One never could. Did Judas
betray you from despair, the hopelessness
deepened till he had no defense against extinction?

A harsh love you showed them,
but still love. A kinder love
might have left them the children they were,
quarreling among themselves about the rules
of the game. You showed them a manhood
so rooted and constant they followed
you toward it—all but one.
They failed. But they came back
to follow again. And you did not
shame them or reject them. Peter
would go on stumbling all his life—
stumbling and returning. This,
not some fantasy of perfection,
is his claim on us.
You held out the hand to him anyway.
You steadied him on the heaving waters of the storm.

XLIII

Holiness

The saints draw our gaze not
to themselves, but to the source of their radiance,
even as each gives varying color
to the light. Bernard in his monastery
struggled with arrogance and a violent
spirit. Is that why he spoke
so compellingly of love? Julian
asked to experience your suffering
and from it learned—what surprises
you know how to work!—hope
and generosity. Hildegard navigated
the twin oceans of nature and music
and found your wisdom flowing in them.

    Heroism may produce greatness
but only holiness is transparent
to your love, a glass wiped clear
by grace so that we, the ordinary
sluggards, can see you there
shining, beckoning. Your deep
mystery arouses love, and we
follow, stumbling and imperfect
as the saints, yet reflecting the first

traces of a dawn that will grow
into full morning.

    To be loved is the beginning of sainthood.
To learn love is its food and stay.
To practice love its delight.
Knowing is of little consequence.
A saint may go about the life
of sainting, the life of transparent
shining, without knowing
the theory of it. Gift,
not knowledge, lives at its heart.

    Gift is surprise is grace.
Your grace touches us when
and where you choose. If we seek it,
we will find it. If we run from it,
it may yet find us. Happy
catastrophe to fall into the embrace
of the lover we had thought to flee
and learn that this is where
we wanted to be all along!

    You offer your hand. You bring us
to the banqueting house. You persuade us
of our beauty and your passion.
You bring us to the marriage feast
and feed us choice morsels
and draw us close to your breast.
Returning your embrace—this
is the root and flower of holiness.

XLIV

The Gift We Need

Can't you make things simpler,
purer for us? Can't you give
certainty in the good and freedom
from evil? Why is our life
such a mix of truth
and lies? Free us! Resolve
our doubts! Rend the heavens!
Come down and make all clear!

    All right, I know it is impossible.
If we didn't dissolve in fear,
we should cripple our brains
trying to see what only you
can see. And our cry for knowledge
is really just a cry for certainty.
Ever since the first parents
discovered they were naked, we've felt
defenseless and ashamed in the world.

    Half of religion is our attempt
to make a system so clear
it would give us security.
It never works.
If it worked, we wouldn't need

to shun or anathematize or kill
the people that don't fit
to prove how right we are.
        Ah, but the other half!
The other half is friendship,
the friendship our first forebears
surrendered in their fear and shame.
The true epiphanies are not
the ones that terrify, driving
us back to our place in the line
of slaves. The true epiphanies,
however deeply they shake
the foundations of our lives, offer
to renew the friendship we fled
so long ago. They invite
us to be loved. They invite us
to love. They invite us to join
in the work whose meaning is love.
        But it's never clear or simple.
You sent Moses into trouble
when he stood unshod before you
as the bush burned and was not consumed.
You sent the prophets to speak
difficult and disruptive truths.
You sent Jesus to offer life
in a world whose chosen weapon
is death. You sent his disciples
to follow him in that.
Mostly, they failed, as we do still.

But the gift we need from you
is not certainty. That will not help.
The gift we need is the reminder
of your love, the hand so long
ignored offered again
in friendship. Only this,
a love renewed again and again,
can give us what we need.

XLV

The Cycle of Death

After the Garden came toil,
hardship, bitterness, and domination
one by another. Fear
and greed drive our world.
Cain found that murder succeeded,
but only for a moment. Then
it turned into a repeating loop,
one murderer never safe
from the next. That hard-won, bloody
knowledge has proven difficult
to pass down through the generations.
We have to discover it again ourselves.

    Sometimes your whole work
seems to have failed, the failure
nowhere more distressing
than in the leagues we form to further it.
Our worst subverts our best.
The godly become demonic.
The community of hope we turn
into one more weapon of dominion.

    Once "faith has been made
to cut the throat of charity,"

faith, too, dies. Or, no,
she was already dead,
replaced by her demonic double.
Only you are faithful.
In our hands, faith keeps turning into
arrogance, bigotry, the violence
of the spirit—all the sins
most favored by piety, the same
that sent you to the cross,
another Abel swept
out of the way in our wars.

    Your disciples began to understand.
Their disciples caught some of it.
But it only takes one generation
out of the Garden to produce
both Abel and Cain. And we cannot
shed them, cannot purge
the murder from our heart.

    We thank you for the moments of return,
moments when you meet us again,
moments when the Garden grows up
once again around us. Without them,
we should lose hope altogether.
Blessed is that meeting
where two or three are gathered
together and you in their midst,
when fear and greed depart,
replaced by quiet joy,
the sharing of food, a readiness

to be friends with you and one another.
Such moments are our only touchstone.
When we fall away from them,
we fall away from you
and from your hopes for us
and from the gift of life
into the cycle of death.

XLVI

Good Shepherd

Seeker, searcher, rescuer
of the strayed, the rejected sheep,
the one driven off by hirelings,
abandoned by the false shepherds
in their long robes with fine embroidery,
you never give us up
for lost. But girding up your loins,
you wade into the thorns,
ignoring the blood on your legs.
You dare the sharp rocks and the snake
concealed in the crevices.
Even if its bite should kill,
you do not cease your work.
You alone are patient,
suffering what you must to accomplish
what you will, to rescue those cast off.

And the guardians of the law, the priests
of religion, the preachers, where
are they? Some of them
follow to help in your work,
some to restrain you, some
to drive off those who dare approach.

It was always so.
Those closest to you tried
to drive the rest away.
They never knew it was you
they drove off.
        Is it possible
that you still seek even them,
even the pious, the priests,
the managers of religion who have stolen
your name and trademarked it?
who stand at the ticket booth
and collect tolls and refuse
all those who cannot pay?
Do you still love,
still seek for them? Can they learn
to enter your household, humbly
following the line of tax-collectors
and prostitutes more willing to be found
by you?
        You didn't come
to save the righteous. We first
must discover that our righteousness
is something else, to see
the sin in which it is rooted.
You saw that religion is itself
the final refuge of sin.
It was we, who thought ourselves faithful,
that tried to kill you. But you live.
You escape our grasp and come

seeking us yet again,
refusing to be frightened off.

    But first you seek the others,
the ones with fewer pretensions,
the ones we tried to keep away.
Blessed are those who make no claim on you,
for they will become your lovers.
Blessed are those who have been cast aside,
for they shall sit at your table.
Blessed are the impure,
for you will share your cup with them.
Blessed are those who long,
for they alone will be filled.
Blessed are they who surrender all confidence in
       their virtue.
Only they will enter the bridal chamber with joy
       and dancing,
their lamps burning, their song never ending,
to take their seats at the banquet of the ages.

    What is our life without your love?
Let worship fall. Let holy places
come to ruin if they no longer point to you.
But let us not lose your love.
Do not cease to seek us
and to find. Do not surrender
to those who would detain you
for the good of religion. Let love
work its will on us and them,
retrieve us, remake us, teach us

to love, as you love, even your enemies
and ours.
       And when we sense you
near us, give us grace
to halt our flight, to receive you
with the kiss of peace and enter
into your embrace. There we shall find ourselves
again renewed, again
called into your own life.
Whatever has been desolate and arid
in our world, watered by your rains,
becomes full of promise
and blossoms anew with lilies
we hadn't known were waiting underground.

XLVII

You

You are the Power that Gives,
you the Creator, you
the Reason that is the Source of All.
You are the Fountain of All Good,
the Beauty that never ceases
to Delight. You are Breath
that brings worlds to Life.
You are Wisdom that reveals
the Hidden. You are Grace-Giver,
Healer, Lover.
   If we say
that yours, too, is the power
to destroy, what more would that tell us?
You are not the slave
of goodness, but its Giver.
You are the Love you serve
as Lover. All power is yours
and you alone are uncorrupted.

 You are Breaker of spells,
so that we see again,
unblinded, the world around us—
Love and Wisdom standing

at either side to interpret.
You are Deliverer from fear,
Dissolver of hatred. You
are the Lancer of old, septic wounds,
the Balm that softens, the Oil
that washes away what is dead,
the Touch that heals. You are the Vision
of New Life. By you we begin
to build instead of destroy.
Following you, we become
creators carried in your wake,
learners of your mysteries,
friends of the Friend and of one another.

    And, no, it is not simple.
Some days are full of pain.
Some days joy awakens
only to be obscured by clouds.
Still, you are Sustainer
of what you have created.
You will complete what you have begun.
You are the Journey that ends in you.

XLVIII

The Age to Come

In the Age to Come, John says,
there is no temple, only you
and the people you have brought home to dinner.
There's no opinion there,
right or wrong, no heresy,
no orthodoxy, only the knowledge
lover has of lover. Right opinion
will find its place in hell,
with all the other murderous
inventions of demonic ingenuity.
Only right praise, the praise
that is the gift of loving lips,
will have a place there. If your lover
is sometimes inept and makes
doggerel for poetry, you smile
and take the intention for the gift,
letting it become another thread
in the great polyphony that makes
the music of the universe, whose first
notes you yourself sang.

    You stand at the door, welcoming
the surprised guests, some of them
protesting that they never met you,

others that they are too flawed,
too dirty to be in this place
of exquisite beauty and delight.
And each you clothe in a new robe
radiant with grace, you wash
the tears from their cheeks, you cleanse
their wounds and bind them up.
And you say, "Remember when
you did this for me?" "Why, no,
but I did it once for someone,
I've forgotten who." "I was there.
It was I. Come now, ye blessed
of my father; inherit the garden
we have made to enjoy with you."

  Some will turn away, too angry
to mingle with the unworthy. They, too, will seek
their own place, a place to be pure,
a place to rule, where currencies
of this world count for something still.
There they will make parties and religions,
theories and wars. They will enforce
their truth on one another,
only to lose the next round
of battle and become subject to their victims.
There will be pimps and loan sharks
there, waging their wars
block by block. There will be
managers and executives, stealing
from one another, and posing

as benefactors of humanity. The brass
of general officers will be seen there
and the garb of religious authorities.
And they will look round in vain
for the poor, the meek, the powerless
they preyed on all those years.
They are nowhere to be found.
They have been welcomed at the gate
of delights and are feasting even now
in the banqueting hall.
                    The true saints
are here. They throng around you
at the door to greet newcomers.
They take each by the hand
and say, "Fear nothing. There is nothing
to fear. Here is the neighbor
you thought was your enemy. That is
over. The real enemies
have only one another to bite
and chew on now. Your moment
of generosity, even if it was but one,
is the germ of your life here."

Taken by the hand with kindness,
we enter into your joy.
And we know we have been here before.
We recognize the fragrance, encountered
before, even if but rarely.
It is the grace made sensible
in a spring day, in a love unearned,

in a stray leap of joy
without cause or explanation.
You have planted signs of it,
seeds of it, everywhere, destined
to grow in us, breaking
the stony soil of frightened
hearts with insistent roots,
searching for the trace of moisture
they know still lies deep down
within.

       And what of the denizens
of hell? Do you dare plant
your seeds even in them?
Is there hope of germination there?
But I forget. You
are the Prodigal One, sowing everywhere.
You do not calculate. You hope.

   Do not give up your hope
or we will fall from ours
and lie like desiccated corpses
in waste places, hedged about by fears,
unable to scent the water
that flows not far away.
Grant us, like Hagar, an angel
who reveals the well. To see you
is life. To lay hold on you
is food and drink for the journey.
To be welcomed by you at the door
is the seal of joy.

XLIX

Journeying

Now near at hand, now seeming
far away, you cannot be anchored
to one spot. Neither book nor altar,
neither shrine nor rite nor icon
can take your place. All
they can do is point—
not even the pointing of a finger
with its suggestion of precision,
but some big gesture, the full
sweep of an arm that signifies
"Over there, in the direction of the hills—
from there your help will come—
or there your journey will take you."
        Trust, hope, love—
these make the journey possible.
We find companions in the writings,
food in the rites, shelter
in the shrine, sometimes a doorway
in the icon. But when courage
fails us, we draw back.
We decide we can stay at home,
that reading the map is as good

as the journey, even though the charts
are tattered, full of gaps,
and leave great stretches of space
unmarked except by fantastic
images of monsters. We tell ourselves
that the wafer is enough, no one
needs the banquet of rich wines.
We make our guides our goal.
The gesture meant to send us out
begins to turn back on itself
and become the beckoning hand
of the idol.

      Help us to raise
our eyes and see the hills
beyond. Free us from fear.
There on the mountain tops,
where you run like a gazelle,
we shall find you. You will lead—
and wait for us—and lead again
till we enter the country of your joy,
watered by streams of life,
planted with trees of healing and delight.

L

Envoi

The morning's autumnal chill,
noisy with crows, will give way
to a warm and sunny afternoon.
Already, the sun is creeping
over the Oakland hills,
the sky a wash of palest
blue, overlaid with gold.

    The year grows old and resigns itself
to a quieter life, even to death.
So be it. You do not prevent
suffering or death, but you call us
to hope. You send your prophets
to release the slaves, to make them
a people, to call us into justice.
You yourself come to woo us
and teach us again to live
in the garden we've long tried
to destroy.

    We live here only
by love, the love of one another,
the love of the whole creation.
From you, the first and final one,

we learn it. From you, the lover
who never falters, we learn
the constancy that can shift the world
onto a different course,
the patience that returns to the work
after disappointment, the courage
to speak and to labor, the love
that set the universe in motion
and sustains it still and guides
us all toward the consummation.

What if it's autumn? You
don't stop working. There's pruning
to be done and the clearing away
of debris. There will be crocuses to watch for,
the beginnings of a new generation.
Perhaps they will hear the lover's
voice and answer and walk with you
on the hills, amid the splendors
of the spring meadows, descending
at the heat of noon to fragrant
shadows along the stream,
there to rest in quiet consummation,
a delight known only to lover and beloved.
Only by hope can we come there.
Only by love will we remain.

Acknowledgments

Jon Vieira listened to the first draft of many of these poems in the evenings, as we prepared dinner. I thank him both for encouragement and for a willingness to say, "That hasn't quite come together yet."

Judith Berling was the first to see some of them in manuscript, and I owe much to her strong encouragement. Barbara Oliver and friends at St. Mark's Berkeley gave "The Tree of Life" its first oral performance. Richard "Red" Stevens was first to read the entire manuscript, and his enthusiasm gave me new confidence in what I had done.

A particular thank you to Davis Perkins, who saw what I was trying to do when I could barely explain it myself and who has championed the work through the process of publication.

Finally, great thanks to Pene Brook for permission to place her work "Wisdom at the Creation of the World" on the cover.

List of Major
References and Sources

Note: Most biblical quotations come from the Authorized (King James) Version or, in the case of Psalms, from the 1928 American *Book of Common Prayer.* Exceptions are noted.

I	Genesis 1:3
II–III	Horace, *Odes* 3.13
	Ovid, *Metamorphoses* 2.1–5 (my translation)
	Euripides, *Hippolytus*
IV	Psalm 104:3
V	Exodus 2–3
VI	1 Samuel 15:3
	Exodus 14:23–31
	Leviticus 18:24–30
VII	Genesis 2:8
	Christina Rossetti, "'To what purpose is this waste?'"
	Genesis 3:14–19; 4; 5:21–24
VIII	Psalm 149:3
IX	Genesis 6–9
X	Jeremiah 18
	C. S. Lewis, *The Great Divorce* (New York: Macmillan, 1946), 8–11.
XI	Genesis 2–3
	Song of Solomon 7:11–12

XL	John 15
	1 John 4
XLI	Exodus 16:19–20
	Psalm 23:5 in the Old Greek version
XLII	Mark 3:13–19
	John 15:16
	Mark 10:32–45
	Matthew 14:22–36
XLIII	Song of Solomon 2:4
XLIV	Genesis 3:7
XLV	Genesis 4
	Jeremy Taylor, *The Great Exemplar*, Discourse VII of Faith, section 12 (referring to the British religious wars of the seventeenth century)
	Matthew 18:20
XLVI	John 10:1–18
	Matthew 18:10–14
	Ezekiel 34
	Matthew 25:31–46
	Matthew 21:31
	Mark 2:17
	Henry Vaughan, "The Revival"
XLVIII	Revelation 21:22–22:7
	George Herbert, "Love (III)"
	Matthew 25:31–46
	Mark 4:1–9
	Genesis 16; 21:8–21
XLIX	Psalm 121
	Song of Solomon 8:14

CPSIA information can be obtained
at www.ICGtesting.com
Printed in the USA
FSOW03n0650101116
27216FS